MONUMENTAL MILESTONES
GREAT EVENTS OF MODERN TIMES

The Story of September 11, 2001

The aftermath of the September 11, 2001, terrorist attack on the World Trade Center.

Mitchell Lane PUBLISHERS

P.O. Box 196
Hockessin, Delaware 19707

Titles in the Series

MONUMENTAL MILESTONES
GREAT EVENTS OF MODERN TIMES

The Story of September 11, 2001

Firefighters Dan McWilliams, George Johnson, and Billy Eisengrein raise the U.S. flag hours after the Twin Towers collapsed.

Kathleen Tracy

Mitchell Lane
PUBLISHERS

Printing   1   2   3   4   5   6   7   8   9

Library of Congress Cataloging-in-Publication Data
Tracy, Kathleen.
 The story of September 11, 2001 / by Kathleen Tracy.
     p. cm. — (Monumental milestones)
 Includes bibliographical references and index.
 ISBN 978-1-58415-693-2 (library bound)
 1. September 11 Terrorist Attacks, 2001. 2. Bin Laden, Osama, 1957– 3. Jihad.
 4. War on Terrorism, 2001– I. Title.
 HV6432.7.T73 2009
 973.931—dc22
                                                                        2008020930

ABOUT THE AUTHOR: Kathleen Tracy has been a journalist for over twenty years. Her writing has been featured in magazines including *The Toronto Star*'s "Star Week," *A&E Biography* magazine, *KidScreen* and *TV Times*. She is also the author of numerous books for Mitchell Lane Publishers, including *William Hewlett: Pioneer of the Computer Age; The Fall of the Berlin Wall; Leonardo da Vinci; Odysseus; The McCarthy Era; The Life and Times of Rosa Parks; Johnny Depp; Mariah Carey;* and *Kelly Clarkson.*

PUBLISHER'S NOTE: This story is based on the author's extensive research, which she believes to be accurate. Documentation of such research is contained on page 46.
    The internet sites referenced herein were active as of the publication date. Due to the fleeting nature of some web sites, we cannot guarantee they will all be active when you are reading this book.

DEDICATION: To all the families and friends who lost a loved one on September 11, 2001

PLB

Contents
The Story of September 11, 2001

Kathleen Tracy

*For Your Information

The first sign of trouble for United Airlines Flight 175 came at 8:42 A.M. when the crew reported hearing a suspicious transmission from American Flight 11.

At 9:03 A.M., Flight 175 crashed into the South Tower. The attack was witnessed by millions of horrified television viewers.

An Unusually Beautiful Day . . .

It was a beautiful late summer morning, the kind of day even busy New Yorkers took a moment to appreciate. The sky was spectacularly clear, tinted an azure blue, the air stirred by a gentle breeze. The mood of the city seemed optimistic as people hurried down the crowded streets on their way to work. Then the world as people knew it forever changed.

8:46 A.M. On the streets of Manhattan, two French brothers, Jules and Gedeon Naudet, were videotaping footage for their documentary about a rookie New York fireman. Gedeon was at a local firehouse. Jules was out with Fire Chief Joe Pfeiffer and some firefighters, checking out a suspected gas leak not far from the Twin Towers. As he held his camera, Jules heard a loud roar overhead. He looked up and instinctively turned the camera toward the sound.

"I had time to see the plane going in between two buildings," Jules said later. "I could even make out *American Airlines* on it, because it was that close."[1] He didn't realize until later that day that he had filmed American Airlines Flight 11 crashing into the World Trade Center's North Tower between the 94th and 98th floors. The impact tore a jagged, gaping hole in the building, shooting out balls of flame and debris. The street shook as if there were an earthquake. The jet fuel fed an intensely hot fire that consumed the planes and any combustibles inside the building. Within minutes, local news crews were rushing to the World Trade Center, broadcasting live footage of what most assumed was a terrible accident. It soon became apparent that this was no accident.

9:03 A.M. As a national audience watched live news coverage of the burning North Tower, United Airlines Flight 175 came into view. Traveling at almost 600 miles per hour and banking sharply, the plane sliced into the South Tower between the 78th and 85th floors. Pieces of the plane exploded out the

north and east sides of the tower, with some of the debris landing as far as six blocks away.

It was obvious this was no accident. New York was under attack, and commercial flights were the weapon of choice. An FAA manager based in New York told the Air Traffic Control System Command Center in Herndon, Virginia: "We have several situations going on here. It's escalating big, big time. We need to get the military involved with us. . . . We have other aircraft that may have a similar situation going on here."[2]

9:15 A.M. NBC's *Today* reported that the American Airlines flight had been hijacked prior to crashing into the North Tower. The Federal Aviation Administration, or FAA, closed all New York area airports, banning all takeoffs and all air traffic in the northeast United States. Minutes later, the Port Authority ordered the closure of all New York area bridges and tunnels.

9:24 A.M. The FAA notified the Northeast Air Defense Sector, also known as NORAD, that American Airlines Flight 77 may have also been com-

Shards of metal, sheets of paper, and human remains rained down on the streets below the World Trade Center after the planes hit.

The plane that hit the South Tower came in lower and at a sharper angle than the plane that struck the North Tower, causing more structural damage and trapping more people above the point of impact. The South Tower collapsed an hour later.

mandeered. Unsure just how many aircraft were involved, the FAA grounded all commercial flights, regardless of their destination. It was the first time in American history that air traffic over U.S. airspace had been totally banned.

9:29 A.M. President George W. Bush, on a public appearance at an elementary school, made his first comments about the situation in New York. He acknowledged to the students and their teachers that America had suffered a national tragedy, then led everyone in a moment of silence. He left the school and boarded Air Force One but did not directly return to Washington, D.C.

9:37 A.M. Flight 77 slammed into the western side of the Pentagon. News footage showed a raging fire, although the damage seemed contained to the impact area. Several newscasts suggested that Saudi militant Osama bin Laden—then still a generally obscure figure—and his Al-Qaeda organization may have been behind the attacks.

9:45 A.M. People on the West Coast awakened to unimaginable news and images from New York and Washington, D.C. Reports that a fourth airliner

The Pentagon is the world's largest office building and the most fortified. Although over 100 people died, the structural soundness of the Pentagon saved countless lives.

When American Airlines Flight 77 crashed into the Pentagon, it was clear this was an attack of unprecedented proportions.

was unaccounted for prompted the evacuation of the Capitol and the White House. Military fighter jets began patrolling the skies along the East Coast, but because Flight 93's transponders were turned off, the plane was essentially invisible to radar.

10:03 A.M. United Airlines Flight 93 crashed in Somerset County, Pennsylvania, southeast of Pittsburgh.

10:05 A.M. Those on the ground at the World Trade Center could feel a massive vibration. Television viewers watched the top of the South Tower shimmy then collapse, seeming to shrink floor by floor as the building pancaked down to the ground. On TV screens, it crumbled in eerie slow motion.

10:24 A.M. The FAA reported that all inbound transatlantic aircraft flying into the United States were being diverted to Canada.

10:28 A.M. The World Trade Center's North Tower collapsed. Outside, emergency crews and evacuees scrambled to avoid being crushed beneath the imploding building. The force of the collapse sent a rushing, suffocating billow

United Airlines Flight 93 crashed in rural Pennsylvania before it could return to Washington, D.C., and hit its designated target.

Flight 93 was the last plane to be hijacked because airport congestion delayed its departure. Forty minutes into the flight, the hijackers overpowered the flight crew and took control of the plane.

of smoke and debris down the narrow downtown streets. Spectators and passersby could not outrun the thick cloud. Some were able to escape into nearby businesses. Those who couldn't find shelter were engulfed.

12:04 P.M. People in Los Angeles International Airport, the original destination for three of the hijacked planes, were evacuated. Minutes later, San Francisco International Airport, the destination of United Airlines Flight 93, was also evacuated and shut down.

1:04 P.M. Speaking from Barksdale Air Force Base in Louisiana, President Bush said that all appropriate security measures were being taken, with the U.S. military on high alert worldwide. Within hours, five warships and two aircraft carriers would embark from U.S. Naval Station Norfolk, in Virginia, to protect the United States from further attack.

2:30 P.M. The FAA announced there would be no U.S. commercial air traffic until Wednesday noon, at the soonest.

It wasn't the impact of the airplanes that caused the Twin Towers to collapse; it was the intense fire caused by the jet fuel that caused the buildings' metal structure to fail.

A half hour after the collapse of the South Tower, the North Tower imploded.

The World Trade Center complex was comprised of seven buildings, three of which collapsed the day of the attacks.

At 5:20 P.M., the 47-story building at 7 World Trade Center collapsed. By then, it was completely evacuated, so there were no casualties. It took three months before the fire in the ruins was completely extinguished.

4:00 P.M. CNN reported that unnamed U.S. officials confirmed there were solid indications that Osama bin Laden, who was also suspected of coordinating the bombings of two U.S. embassies in 1998, was involved in the attacks, based on information uncovered over the course of the day.

4:10 P.M. Building 7 of the World Trade Center complex, which was severely damaged when the North and South Towers fell, was reported to be on fire. An hour later, the forty-seven-story structure collapsed.

7:45 P.M. The New York Police Department reported that at least 78 officers were missing. City officials feared half of the first 400 firefighters on the scene were killed.

Over the next two days, four thousand FBI agents were enlisted to work on what was called the most massive criminal investigation ever conducted in America. Not since Pearl Harbor had America's security been so catastrophically breached. This time, however, the enemy wasn't a country with an opposing political philosophy. It was an individual and his followers whose hatred of America was based on militant religious beliefs. Before September 11, 2001, few people knew of Osama bin Laden. After the attack on the World Trade Center, bin Laden would become a household name and public enemy number one.

The idea for the World Trade Center was first proposed in the early 1950s as part of an effort to gentrify lower Manhattan. The idea was conceived by the Downtown-Lower Manhattan Development Association, which had been founded by Chase Manhattan Bank Chairman David Rockefeller. David and his brother, New York governor Nelson Rockefeller, strongly supported the construction, believing it would benefit the entire city.

The Port Authority of New York and New Jersey began the planning stage for the World Trade Center in 1962. Michigan architectural firm Yamasaki and Associates was hired to design the complex. Minoru Yamasaki envisioned two huge towers, but the idea was originally met with some skepticism. Critics complained that it would destroy New York's famous skyline. Others worried it would interfere with television reception. There was also some concern that the buildings' sheer size would strain city resources. Despite

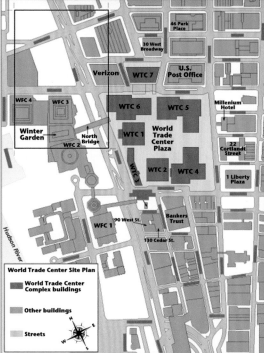

these reservations, the project was approved and construction on the towers began in 1966.

To create the 16-acre complex, five streets were closed and over 160 buildings torn down. More than one million cubic yards of earth was excavated. A total of ten thousand people worked on the towers in some capacity; sixty of them died during the building.

The North Tower opened in December 1970; the South Tower fourteen months later, in January 1972. They were the world's tallest buildings until Sears Tower in Chicago was completed in May 1973.

In addition to the two main towers, there were four other office buildings and a hotel built around the central plaza of the World Trade Center complex. Beneath the plaza were a mall, two subway terminals, and a train depot. Approximately 50,000 people worked in the buildings, and on average, another 200,000 visitors passed through daily. In many ways, the World Trade Center was its own city. It even had its own zip code: 10048.

Osama bin Laden founded Al-Qaeda in 1988 to advance the Islamic revolution he was envisioning.

Bin Laden was born in Saudi Arabia, where his father was a billionaire businessman. As a young man, he traveled to Afghanistan and joined other Muslim fighters who succeeded in ending the Soviet Union's occupation of the country.

The Making of a Terrorist

The first time *The New York Times* wrote about Osama bin Laden was in 1994. In a story examining Sudan's support of Islamic militant groups, bin Laden is mentioned in passing. He has been described as a "wealthy Saudi financier who bankrolls Islamic militant groups from Algeria to Saudi Arabia."[1] The paper ran a more in-depth profile of bin Laden two years later, singling out him and his group, Al-Qaeda, as a primary threat to America and other Western nations. Even so, he operated in virtual anonymity. It was only after September 11 that bin Laden's shadowy life was thrust fully into the public spotlight.

Osama bin Laden was born in 1957 into one of Saudi Arabia's wealthiest families. He was the seventeenth of twenty-four sons. The bin Ladens were immigrants. Osama's father, Mohammed Awad bin Laden, came to Saudi Arabia from Yemen in 1932. He was friends with Saudi King Abdul Aziz al-Saud and through the king was contracted to build roads and renovate shrines in Mecca and Medina. The work made Mohammed extremely wealthy. In 1968, he died in a plane crash while in Texas. Although nobody knows exactly how much inheritance Osama received, it is believed it was at least $20 million. Mohammed's company, the Saudi Binladen Group, continued, and by 2008 employed 35,000 people and had over $5 billion in assets. Osama would receive a substantial monthly stipend from the company's profits.

Because of the inheritance, Osama grew up independently wealthy. He and his family were members of the Wahhabi sect of Sunni Muslims, a very conservative group that holds beliefs not followed by other Muslims. Wahhabi is considered to be the primary Islamic religious movement behind extremism. Although Osama studied Islam, as a young man he also enjoyed the trappings of his wealth. He would fly to Beirut to gamble and find women to date. More than once the six-foot-five-inch teenager got into fights.

When he was eighteen, Osama enrolled in King Abdul Aziz University. He majored in civil engineering and planned to join the family business. While at college, he began listening to lectures by Abdullah Azzam, who belonged to the Muslim Brotherhood, an ultraconservative group that promoted extremist beliefs. Azzam had a profound influence on bin Laden, and his teachings deepened Osama's religious beliefs. It also encouraged him to become more personally involved in promoting Islam.

In 1979, the same year bin Laden graduated, the Soviet Union invaded Afghanistan. He saw the invasion as a direct assault against Islam and an offense against God. He also viewed the Afghan resistance as a kind of holy war. He raised vast sums of money for the Afghan fighters, known as mujahideen, and donated millions of his own. He used equipment from his family's business to build roads, tunnels, and camps for the Afghan resistance.

"He's not very sophisticated politically or organizationally," said a former bin Laden associate known as Abdullah Anas. "But he's an activist with great imagination. He ate very little. He slept very little. He'd give you his clothes. He'd give you his money."[2]

In 1984, bin Laden moved to Pakistan, where he and his mentor Azzam formed the group Maktab Al-Khidamat (Office of Services). It is also known as Al-Kifah (The Struggle). In addition to recruiting and training Muslim volunteers from countries throughout the Middle East to fight in the Afghan war, the group also served as a fund-raising entity. Branches of Maktab Al-Khidamat opened in over 30 U.S. cities, and Muslim-Americans donated millions of dollars to support the Afghan war against the Soviet Union. The most important branch was the Al-Kifah Refugee Center in Brooklyn, New York.

Azzam wanted Maktab Al-Khidamat to devote itself exclusively to the fight against the Soviets in Afghanistan. But Osama believed there was a bigger war to fight—preventing Western influences from corrupting Muslim countries. One of the groups committed to spreading Islam through terrorism and violence was the Egyptian Islamic Jihad, which participated in the assassination of Egyptian President Anwar Sadat in 1981. One of the group's leaders, Ayman al-Zawahiri, became one of bin Laden's closest associates.

In 1986, bin Laden established a training camp for fifty men. He named the camp Al Masadah, or "the lion's den." Osama and Azzam eventually parted ways, and the Maktab Al-Khidamat organization split. In 1988, bin Laden

Like bin Laden, al-Zawahiri came from a prominent family but turned militant at a young age. After 9/11, the U.S. Department of State offered a $25 million reward for information leading to al-Zawahiri's apprehension or conviction.

Egypt-born surgeon Ayman al-Zawahiri was considered Osama bin Laden's right-hand man.

formed a new group with the Egyptians called Al-Qaeda, which means "The Base." A year later, Azzam was assassinated. That same year, the Soviets pulled out of Afghanistan, which bin Laden and other extremists considered a major victory.

Buoyed by the successful ouster of the occupying Soviets, Osama and his peers set out to apply the same principals of jihad, or holy war, to advance fundamental Islam. Even though the Qur'an strictly limits when a holy war can be waged, bin Laden and other extremists do not follow the mainstream interpretation of the Islamic holy book. Instead, they justify their violence by embracing a radical interpretation of the Qur'an. After Azzam's death, Maktab Al-Khidamat essentially became an arm of Al-Qaeda and would be used to make the concept of a global holy war a reality.

When he went back to Saudi Arabia, bin Laden became outraged when King Fahd allowed American troops into the country to use as a base of operations during the 1991 Persian Gulf War. Not only were the U.S. soldiers fighting

other Arabs, they brought their music, social beliefs and—compared to fundamentalist Islam—liberal attitudes. In his view, America used its power to repress Muslims and was an enemy because it supported Israel. After a brief stay in Afghanistan, bin Laden moved to the Sudan in 1991. He chose that country because of its Islamic government.

In some ways, bin Laden ran his militant organization like a corporation. Al-Qaeda was very organized and was financed through traditional investments as well as outside support. Under bin Laden's leadership, Al-Qaeda began a campaign of violence against the Western world. He supported Islamic revolutions and the complete elimination of Western influence in the Middle East—and beyond. His goal was to have an organization with a global reach so that he could promote his extreme form of Islam around the world.

In 1994, his native Saudi Arabia revoked his citizenship. His family disowned him, cutting off his monthly stipend. Mainstream Islamic leaders renounced Osama because he used Islam to justify killing. The U.S. government labeled him a stateless sponsor of terrorism and pressured Sudan to deport him. In 1996, he was expelled from Sudan and returned to Afghanistan, where the militant Islamic government of the Taliban welcomed him. The Taliban also allowed bin Laden to set up training camps that attracted young Muslim men from all across the Middle East. In Afghanistan they were trained to use explosives and other weapons, and they were schooled in spy tactics.

For the first several years after forming, Al-Qaeda operated under the radar, not attracting the attention of U.S. intelligence services as it trained fighters and set up its network. Then in December 1992, a bomb went off at a hotel in Yemen. Although only two Austrian tourists were killed, it was believed that the intended victims were U.S. soldiers in Yemen on their way to Somalia as part of a humanitarian and peacekeeping mission. Two Muslims from Yemen, who trained in Afghanistan, were eventually arrested for their part in the bombing. It is now believed this was Al-Qaeda's first attack.

What is most ironic is that for a while, bin Laden was technically a U.S. ally when America was assisting the Afghan mujahideen against the Soviets. But by the late 1990s, it had become clear that Osama bin Laden was one of the Western world's most dangerous enemies.

Allah is our objective. The Prophet is our leader. Qur'an is our law. Jihad is our way. Dying in the way of Allah is our highest hope.[3] —Muslim Brotherhood

The Muslim Brotherhood was founded in 1928 by a twenty-two-year-old Egyptian elementary schoolteacher named Hasan al-Banna. He believed that Islam was not simply a set of religious practices or rituals but represented a political and social culture. He also promoted jihad against non-Muslims.

Hasan al-Banna

The Brotherhood gained in popularity throughout the Arab world and used terrorism to promote its ideals, which was to run the government under Islamic law. Egypt banned the Brotherhood as a political entity, allowing it to exist only as a religious group. That did little to curb the Brotherhood's political aspirations. In December 1948, a Muslim Brother assassinated the Prime Minister of Egypt. Two months later, in February 1949, al-Banna was killed by government agents in Cairo. In 1954 a Brother named Abdul Munim Abdul Rauf attempted to assassinate Egyptian President Gamal Abdal Nasser. He failed, and was arrested and executed along with five other Brothers. After that, the Egyptian government permanently banned the group. Four thousand Brothers were arrested in the government crackdown. Thousands of others fled to neighboring countries, including Syria, Saudi Arabia, Jordan, and Lebanon.

Hoping to promote peace, in 1964 President Nasser granted amnesty to Brothers in custody. The gesture backfired, and the group tried three more times to kill Nasser. In turn, the government went after the Brotherhood, executing several of its leaders in 1966 and sending many others to prison. But others took their place. Nasser's successor, Anwar Sadat, earned the group's ire when he signed the historic peace agreement between Egypt and Israel. Two years later, in 1981, four Brothers assassinated Sadat.

The Brotherhood remains active today. Although Egypt is still considered its base, it is estimated there are over seventy branches of the organization worldwide, including Hamas in Palestine. But perhaps the Brotherhood's most important legacy is that it is considered by some experts to be the parent organization of Al-Qaeda.

On February 26, 1993, a car bomb was [...]
parking structure below the North Tow[...]

*The terrorists' plan was
to topple the North Tower
into the South Tower and
destroy both buildings.
While the blast killed six
and injured over 1,000,
the structural damage
to the North Tower was
relatively minimal.*

Jihad

On February 26, 1993, a truck bomb filled with cyanide gas exploded in the parking garage of the World Trade Center. The intent of the terrorists was to undermine the building's foundation so that it would fall over and destroy the other tower while releasing the poisonous gas. Had the plot unfolded as planned, it could have killed over 20,000 people. The tower was able to withstand the blast better than the plotters anticipated, and the heat from the explosion incinerated the deadly gas. In the end six people were killed and hundreds injured, but authorities realized just how much worse it could have been.

New York Governor Mario Cuomo said, "We all have that feeling of being violated. No foreign people or force has ever done this to us. Until now we were invulnerable."[1]

Investigators working the case identified several suspects, including Ramzi Yousef, who was subsequently named the mastermind behind the plot. Yousef and his coconspirators were eventually convicted. The investigation also revealed that the perpetrators were linked to the Al-Kifah Refugee Center in Brooklyn. Since Azzam's death, bin Laden supporters had used that and other Office of Service branches as fund-raising operations for Al-Qaeda. Despite bin Laden's ties to Al-Kifah, however, there was no conclusive proof that he was directly involved in the bombing. Even so, officials believed that at the very least he had helped finance the operation.

While the outcome had been a failure from the terrorists' perspective, it only served to strengthen their resolve. If a car bomb wouldn't bring down the Twin Towers, the terrorists would find something that would. The scope of their plots became increasingly sophisticated. In 1995, Philippine police uncovered a plot with the code name *bojinka,* or "big bang," that called for the explosion of twelve airplanes flying to the United States from Southeast Asia. Authorities

Ramzi   Mohammad   Abdul
Yousef   Salameh   Yasin

Mahmoud   Ahmed   Nidal   Eyad
Abouhalima   Ajaj   Ayyad   Ismoil

The mastermind behind the 1993 bombing was Ramzi Yousef. Along with six co-conspirators, he was charged with carrying out the bombing.

In March 1994, four of the co-conspirators— Ajaj, Abouhalima, Ayyad and Salameh—were convicted. In November 1997, Yousef and Ismoil were also convicted. Abdul Yasin remained on the FBI's Most Wanted Terrorists List.

discovered documents linking Yousef to the plan. One of his associates told investigators that Yousef had discussed hijacking a commercial aircraft and flying it into CIA headquarters. They also talked about possibly using a small airplane loaded with explosives to bomb targets in the United States. The master at plotting possible attacks was Al-Qaeda associate Khalid Shaikh Mohammed, who happened to be related to Ramzi Yousef.

Raised in Kuwait, Khalid saw America as an enemy because of its support for Israel. He joined the Muslim Brotherhood when he was sixteen and attended the group's youth camps. Educated in the United States, he graduated from North Carolina A&T University in 1986 with a degree in mechanical engineering. From there he went to Afghanistan to fight against the Soviets. It is now known that he wired money to one of Yousef's accomplices to support the World Trade Center bombing. He also worked with Yousef on Project Bojinka and was indicted in 1996 as a conspirator in the United States, making him a

3

fugitive. Around that time, Khalid approached Osama bin Laden with a new idea for targeting the World Trade Center.

In February 1998, Al-Qaeda formed a coalition with other extremist groups, including al-Zawahiri's Egyptian Islamic Group. They called themselves the International Islamic Front for Jihad Against the Jews and Crusaders. Bin Laden, still based in Taliban-ruled Afghanistan, was elected the head of the Front's council. One of his first acts was to issue a fatwa that called for Muslims everywhere to kill Americans anywhere in the world: "We—with God's help—call on every Muslim who believes in God and wishes to be rewarded to comply with God's order to kill the Americans and plunder their money wherever and whenever they find it. We also call on Muslim ulema, leaders, youths, and soldiers to launch the raid on Satan's U.S. troops and the devil's supporters allying with them, and to displace those who are behind them so that they may learn a lesson."[2]

In his view, America's crimes were its military presence in Saudi Arabia, being an ally to Israel, and participating in the Persian Gulf War—in which a coalition of 35 countries organized by the United Nations forced Iraqi troops out of Kuwait.

After bin Laden's missive, Al-Qaeda stepped up the number of attacks. In August 1998, it was responsible for bombing U.S. embassies in Kenya and Tanzania that killed more than 200 people, including a dozen Americans. Then in October 2000, Al-Qaeda bombed the destroyer USS *Cole* while it was in port at Aden, Yemen. Seventeen American servicemen were killed. But these bombings were simply a lead-up to Al-Qaeda's most ambitious plot to date, because by early 1999, bin Laden had approved Mohammed Khalid's new plan targeting the World Trade Center.

What makes Al-Qaeda so dangerous is that it is well funded, well organized, and its leaders learn from their mistakes. For example, in December 1994, an Algerian-based terrorist group allied with bin Laden hijacked an Air France plane. The goal was to fly it into the Eiffel Tower. The problem was that none of the hijackers could fly. Instead, the Air France pilot landed the plane in Marseilles, where police captured the hijackers. This time, Khalid made sure his operatives would be much better prepared. They quietly began enrolling in flight schools to learn how to fly commercial jetliners. While it didn't go completely unnoticed, in most cases it didn't set off any urgent alarms.

In July 2001, Kenneth Williams, an FBI agent in Phoenix, Arizona, sent a memo detailing a pattern of young Arab men enrolling at flight schools. He suggested the bureau investigate to see if any of the men were known Al-Qaeda members. No one acted on Williams' memo.

In Eagan, Minnesota, however, someone did take notice when a stocky man with a French accent named Zacarias Moussaoui showed up at the Pan Am Flying Academy. Although he admitted the biggest plane he'd ever flown was a single-engine Cessna, he insisted on being trained on a 747 flight simulator. Specifically, he wanted to learn how to turn the plane in midair. He had no interest in takeoffs or landings. One of the instructors sensed something was off and contacted federal authorities. Moussaoui was taken into custody on August 16 for having an expired visa and was still in jail when nineteen Al-Qaeda associates put the plan to hijack four airliners into motion.

On the morning of September 11, five men waited to board American Airlines Flight 11 at Boston's Logan International Airport. Sometime between 6:45 and 7:40, Mohamed Atta, Abdul Aziz al-Omari, Satam al-Suqami, Wail al-Shehri, and Waleed al-Shehri boarded the plane, which was bound for Los Angeles. The plane took off at 7:59. On board were nine flight attendants and eighty-one passengers. At 8:14, the pilot acknowledged a message from the air traffic control center. Sixteen seconds later, ATC instructed the pilot to take the plane to 35,000 feet. There was no response to that message or to any other attempts to contact the plane. At 8:27, the plane made an unscheduled turn south. . . .

While air traffic controllers were trying to reach Flight 11, in another Logan International Airport terminal, United Airlines Flight 175 to Los Angeles was boarding. A ticket agent later remembered that two of the passengers seemed unused to flying because they had trouble understanding the standard security questions asked when checking in. Other than that, team leader Marwan al-Shehri and his four associates—Fayez Banihammad, Mohand al-Shehri, Ahmed al-Ghamdi, and Hamza al-Ghamdi—were passed through without raising undue suspicions. They joined the nine crew members and fifty-six passengers, and Flight 175 took off at 8:14. At 8:42, the crew reported a suspicious transmission they had overheard coming from another plane—which turned out to be Flight 11. That was the cockpit's last transmission.

Five minutes later, the aircraft changed beacon codes twice within a minute, then deviated from its assigned altitude. At 8:52, New York air traffic controllers tried repeatedly, and unsuccessfully, to contact the aircraft. . . .

The first American Airline flight to Los Angeles out of Dulles Airport near Washington, D.C., was scheduled to take off shortly after 8:00. The first two hijackers to check in for Flight 77 were Khalid al-Mihdhar and Majed Moqed. A short time later, Hani Hanjour and brothers Nawaf al-Hazmi and Salem al-Hazmi also checked in. Of the five, Hanjour, Mihdhar, and Moqed were flagged by the Computer Assisted Passenger Prescreening System, or CAPPS, a security profiling system. The Hazmi brothers were also selected for extra scrutiny at the check-in counter because one of them did not have adequate identification, had trouble understanding English, and both men seemed suspicious to the agent. The only consequence of the security check was that their luggage was not put on the plane until after the men boarded. At the time, security agents were most concerned about bombs aboard the plane. The idea that the plane itself could be used as a bomb was not a concern.

When Mihdhar and Moqed walked through the metal detector, they set off the alarm. After being checked by the hand wand, they passed inspection. Nawaf al-Hazmi also set off the alarm and was also passed through after the wand scan. Security video that was screened later showed Hazmi had something in his back pocket. Once they cleared security, the men boarded Flight 77, which was carrying four flight attendants and 58 passengers. The plane took off at 8:20. By 8:51, Flight 77 had reached its cruising altitude of 35,000 feet and made its final transmission to ATC. Within the next three minutes, the hijackers took over the cockpit, because at 8:54 the aircraft made an unscheduled turn south. Two minutes later the transponder was turned off and radar contact with the aircraft was lost. . . .

Newark International Airport in New Jersey is one of three that service New York City. United Airlines Flight 93 to San Francisco carried a crew of seven and only thirty-seven passengers, including four hijackers: Saeed al-Ghamdi, Ahmed al-Nami, Ahmad al-Haznawi, and Ziad Jarrah. Investigators would later suggest that Zacarias Moussaoui was supposed to be the fifth team member. Once again CAPPS flagged one of the men. Haznawi's bag was screened for explosives, and after coming up negative, it was loaded on the

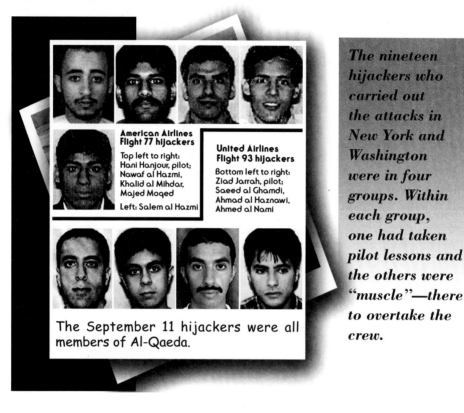

American Airlines Flight 77 hijackers

Top left to right: Hani Hanjour, pilot; Nawaf al Hazmi, Khalid al Mihdar, Majed Moqed

Left: Salem al Hazmi

United Airlines Flight 93 hijackers

Bottom left to right: Ziad Jarrah, pilot; Saeed al Ghamdi, Ahmad al Haznawi, Ahmed al Nami

The September 11 hijackers were all members of Al-Qaeda.

The nineteen hijackers who carried out the attacks in New York and Washington were in four groups. Within each group, one had taken pilot lessons and the others were "muscle"—there to overtake the crew.

plane. Although scheduled to leave the gate at 8:00, there was unusually heavy air traffic and takeoff was delayed until 8:42, just minutes before the first plane flew into the North Tower.

It wasn't until after the second plane plowed into the South Tower that United sent a warning to all its pilots to beware of cockpit intrusion and informed them about the World Trade Center attacks. At 9:26, Flight 93 pilot Jason Dahl asked ATC to confirm their warning. Two minutes later, the hijackers took over the plane, which abruptly dropped 700 feet. During its descent, the FAA air traffic control center in Cleveland received a Mayday transmission. Sounds of a struggle could be heard in the background. A second transmission came 35 seconds later—the sounds of fighting were ongoing, but the cockpit crew was ultimately killed.

Ziad Jarrah, the team member trained to pilot the 757, took over the controls and turned the jetliner around and headed back east. In New York City, the horror had only begun.

The Computer Assisted Passenger Prescreening System, or CAPPS, is an airline security system. It works by analyzing the known information about a passenger, such as type of ticket and method of payment. Based on that information, the computer gives each passenger a score. Those who receive a certain score get extra screening. As originally conceived, now known as CAPPS I, airport security agents concentrated on only a certain selection of passengers so as not to inconvenience the majority of passengers.

CAPPS I was first used in the late 1990s. It was a response to increased concerns over air travel safety in the wake of incidents such as the explosion of TWA Flight 800 on July 17, 1996, and the bombing ten days later in Atlanta's Centennial Olympic Park during the Summer Olympic Games. The FBI and the FAA administered CAPPS I. Passengers selected by CAPPS had their luggage screened for explosives, but the passengers themselves did not receive additional screening. On September 11, eight of the nineteen hijackers were selected by CAPPS; two others were stopped by counter clerks when checking in. Since none of them was carrying explosives, they avoided extra scrutiny. After September 11, new security measures were implemented at airports to make the system more effective against terrorism. Now the U.S. Transportation Security Administration (TSA) has the legal authority to keep a "watch list" of "individuals known to pose, or suspected of posing, a risk of air piracy or terrorism or a threat to airline or passenger safety."[3] The list is used to profile passengers as a way of identifying potential terrorists. A new CAPPS system, CAPPS II, was also planned, but it was highly controversial. When implemented, it would require travelers to give birth date, home address, and other personal information before boarding a flight. Security officials would check the information against government databases. The passenger would then be "tagged" with a color-coded score that indicated how much of a security risk that individual posed. Depending on the score, the person could be questioned, detained, or even prevented from flying. In the end, CAPPS II was scrapped, although work on developing a new automated passenger screening system continued.

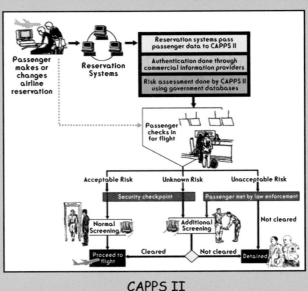

CAPPS II

Of those who died on September 11, at l[...] either in the towers or on the ground.

Among the fatalities in the towers were 343 firefighters, 23 New York City police officers, and 37 Port Authority police officers. Even after the debris was cleared, over 20 people remained officially missing.

Uncommon Heroism

While TV newscasts struggled to keep the nation informed of the ongoing events, countless stories of individual courage and heroism were unfolding inside the planes, the World Trade Center, and the Pentagon as ordinary citizens found themselves thrust into extraordinary circumstances.

Aboard American Airlines Flight 11, the hijackers forced the passengers and crew to the back of the plane. Daniel Levin, a former soldier in the Israeli military, tried to stop Atta and al-Omari from entering the cockpit. He didn't realize another member of the team, al-Suqami, was in the row behind him. The hijacker stabbed Levin. Flight attendant Betty Ong contacted the airline's Southeastern Reservations Office via an air phone, and attendant Madeline "Amy" Sweeney sent reports to manager Michael Woodward in the American Flight Services Office in Boston about what was happening. They also relayed the seat numbers of the hijackers, allowing authorities to get their identities.

While on the phone, Woodward asked Sweeney if she could tell where the plane was. Sweeney looked out the window and told him, "We are flying low. We are flying very, very low. We are flying way too low. . . . Oh my God we are way too low."[1]

The phone call ended as Flight 11 crashed into the North Tower. All three stairwells in the tower were destroyed by the impact, making evacuation of the upper floors impossible. Nobody on those floors survived. Those who were not killed by fire or smoke died when the tower collapsed. Those below the point of impact scrambled to get out of the building, but many still took the time to help others. Workers tore off their shirts to use as bandages for those wounded by the explosion and resulting fire. The healthy assisted the injured down the stairwells to safety. Through all the chaos, hundreds of firefighters and police-men were running into the building to rescue those inside.

After the North Tower was hit, an announcement was made in the South Tower that the building was secure and there was no need to evacuate. But Aon Corporation employee Eric Eisenberg insisted everyone leave their offices, which were on the 98th floor of the South Tower. Fellow employee Marissa Panigrosso remembered, "Eric was very take charge, like let's get moving here. He was the wake up voice. . . . He started the train and then went back for other people."[2]

Sarah Dechalus was one of those people. "Eric passed me. 'Start going down the stairs,' he said. It was a huge floor. He was going around, to the other side. 'Be calm, don't run. We are going to get down safely.' He was concerned about others and went completely around the floor to make sure everyone was getting out."[3]

Thanks to his efforts, Sarah, Marissa, and all the other employees who had left the Aon office were able to reach safety before United Flight 175 plowed into the South Tower. Eisenberg did not survive.

Distraught New Yorkers watched the drama unfold from the streets of lower Manhattan.

Shortly after 10:00, the United Nations was evacuated. The Port Authority of New York and New Jersey ordered all bridges and tunnels in the New York area closed. In Washington, all federal office buildings were cleared.

Structurally, the South Tower was more critically damaged than the North Tower. Architect Bob Shelton, who was wearing a cast on his broken foot, had been on the 56th floor of the South Tower when the plane struck. As he evacuated down the stairwell, he said, "You could hear the building cracking. It sounded like when you have a bunch of spaghetti, and you break it in half to boil it. . . . It was structural failure. Once a building like that is off center, that's it." As Sheldon and the others continued down the stairs, cracks began appearing in the walls and the building seemed to shudder. But, he says, "There was no panic. We were working as a team, helping everyone along the way. Someone carried my crutches, and I supported myself on the railing."[4]

Once people got to the street level, they were confronted with unimaginable horror. Human remains littered the street, along with a blizzard of debris. One man was killed when someone who had jumped from the burning tower landed on him. Police and other city personnel directed people to get away

New York City hospitals were put on high alert, expecting a rush of patients. But the emergency rooms remained largely quiet because nearly all those still in the towers when they collapsed were killed.

New York City Mayor Rudolph Giuliani urged New Yorkers to stay at home.

from the building as fast as they could as more and more firefighters streamed onto the scene.

With the nation's shocked eyes turned to New York, America's capital also came under attack when American Airlines Flight 77 slammed into the Pentagon at 530 miles per hour. The impact breached the three outermost rings of the building. But the design of the building—five concentric rings of concrete surrounding a central courtyard—helped contain the damage and limit fatalities. It also made evacuation easier as military and civilian personnel ran through the halls, telling everyone to get out. The jet-fuel fire incinerated everything in its path and spread along the wooden roof, but firefighters were able to contain the blaze within a few hours.

Although all 64 people on the plane and another 125 in the Pentagon died, the tragedy could have been much worse. The Pentagon, which had been upgraded after the 1995 bombing of the Alfred P. Murrah Federal Building in Oklahoma City, was able to withstand the force of the impact much better than

The fire at the Pentagon was extinguished within a few hours. The design of the building facilitated evacuations.

On September 11, 2008, the Pentagon Memorial was dedicated, honoring the 184 people who were killed in the attack. Each unit of the memorial is dedicated to a specific individual, organized from the youngest to the oldest victim.

the Twin Towers. In fact, some of the people who worked there didn't even know a plane had crashed into the building until they were evacuated.

The Twin Towers, though, had been mortally wounded. Each building had 244 steel girders that formed the perimeter of each floor. Those girders are what gave the towers their structural strength; but between the fire and the damage caused by the impact of the planes, that structural integrity was compromised.

The protocol for high-rise fires has three parts: first, to evacuate everyone beneath the fire. From the Twin Towers, it is estimated that of the approximately 16,000 people who were below the impact zones, 14,000 were successfully evacuated. The next priority is to contain the fire and keep it from spreading down. The last step is to find a way up to rescue those above the impact zone. For those on the top floors, the response teams ran out of time.

As the most heavily burned floors gave way, the floors above them also fell. Their combined weight was too much for the floors beneath the burn area

The dust was made up of pulverized concrete, glass, fiberglass, and human remains. Residents of the area suffered health effects such as coughing and eye and throat irritations.

At 10:28 the North Tower collapsed. The collapse of the towers covered lower Manhattan with a choking cloud of dust.

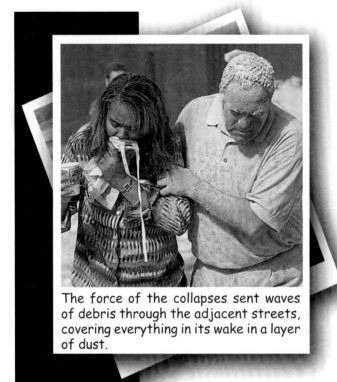

The force of the collapses sent waves of debris through the adjacent streets, covering everything in its wake in a layer of dust.

A 42-year-old attorney named Felicia Dunn-Jones died five months after breathing dust caused by the collapse of the South Tower. Authorities added her name to the official list of World Trade Center victims.

to handle. They also buckled, and the building caved in on itself as floor after floor gave way to the weight crashing down from above. It took less than ten seconds for the South Tower to collapse, crushing vehicles and people unable to get out of the way. The North Tower came down 23 minutes later.

Although local hospitals had all available personnel ready to treat the injured, only a relatively small number of patients arrived. It brought home the terrible reality that of those still in and close to the buildings, very, very few survived. The fatalities included twenty-three New York City police officers, thirty-seven Port Authority police officers, and 343 firefighters and paramedics.

FYInfo
FOR YOUR INFORMATION

The Pentagon is the headquarters for the U.S. Department of Defense. Located in Arlington, Virginia, it is one of the world's largest office buildings. It has three times the floor space of the Empire State Building and over seventeen miles of hallway. More than 23,000 military and civilian employees work at the Pentagon.

The idea for the Pentagon came from Brigadier General Brehon Somervell as a way to solve the War Department's severe lack of office space. Instead of building multiple buildings, Somervell thought a single, massive structure would be more efficient. It was an ambitious, very expensive proposition. Congress appropriated $83 million—the equivalent of $1.2 *billion* in 2008's dollars—for the project.

The first land chosen for the project was a parcel known as Arlington Farms. The site was bordered by five roadways. The layout prompted designer George Bergstrom's distinctive pentagonal shape of the building. But some people worried that the structure would obstruct the view of Washington, D.C., from Arlington National Cemetery, so President Franklin Delano Roosevelt had the building site moved almost a mile away to an area called Hell's Bottom. The five-sided shape was kept, and the final design called for a large open-air court surrounded by five concentric rings connected by ten spoke-like corridors. Despite the size, the corridor design made it possible to walk between any two points of the Pentagon in seven minutes, making it one of the most efficient office buildings in the world.

The groundbreaking ceremony took place on September 11, 1941. Construction was completed in just sixteen months. At its peak, 15,000 workers toiled literally around the clock in three shifts, using floodlights to work at night. The Pentagon was finished on January 15, 1943. The man in charge of overseeing the construction, Colonel Leslie Groves, would be promoted to Lieutenant General and go on to head the Manhattan Project.

The Pentagon enabled the Department of Defense to consolidate seventeen buildings. As a result, it paid for itself after just seven years.

Aerial view of the Pentagon in 2000

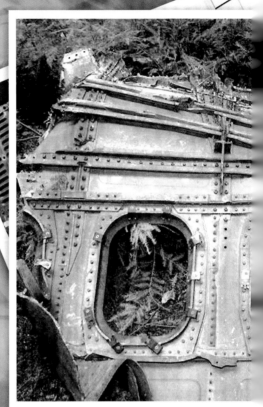

Flight 93 hit the ground with such force found more than a mile away from the

By the time the hijackers took control of Flight 93, several passengers on the plane were aware of the attacks on New York. Authorities believe a passenger revolt prevented the hijackers from fulfilling their mission and forced them to put the plane down in the Pennsylvania field.

Fighting Back

Through cell phone calls to friends and loved ones, the passengers aboard the last hijacked plane, United Airlines Flight 93, learned about the attacks on the World Trade Center and then the Pentagon. It seemed obvious their plane was going to be used as a flying bomb. Rather than go meekly, the passengers decided to fight back. They could not let the plane be used to kill others. They took a vote and agreed: They were going to overtake the hijackers—or die trying.

They were led by a group of defiant and determined young men. Mark Bingham was a six-foot-five-inch graduate of the University of California, Berkeley, who played amateur rugby. Jeremy Glick was six feet four and a national collegiate judo champion. Thomas Burnett was a six-foot-one-inch former high school football player. Todd Beamer was a natural athlete who once considered playing professional baseball. All were successful and charismatic. As events unfolded, they naturally gravitated toward one another.

The atmosphere was tense. At least one person had already been killed, others injured. The plane was flying erratically as hijacker Ziad Jarrah struggled to control the jetliner. While the lead group prepared to rush the cockpit, many of the passengers called loved ones to say good-bye.

"I know we're all going to die," Tom Burnett told his wife, Deena. "There's three of us who are going to do something about it."[1]

Glick's last words to his wife were: "We're going to rush the hijackers."[2] Then he put down the phone.

Todd Beamer had reached a GTE operator named Lisa D. Jefferson by air phone and told her, "We're going to do something." Then he admitted he did not believe he would survive the ordeal and asked Jefferson to tell his wife and two sons that he loved them. Beamer then asked Jefferson to pray with

Firefighters on the scene. The smoke is so thick, they can hardly see or breathe.

Steel I-beams punctuate the debris from the Twin Towers.

President George W. Bush makes a speech at Ground Zero on September 14.

Candlelight vigils were held by thousands, including students at Mary Washington College in Virginia.

A newsboy holds up two newspapers dated September 13, 2001—two days after the 9/11 attacks.

A mother and daughter mourn at Ground Zero on October 30, 2001.

THIS MEMORIAL IS IN MEMORY
OF THE BRAVE MEN AND WOMEN
WHO GAVE THEIR LIVES
TO SAVE SO MANY OTHERS.
THEIR COURAGE AND LOVE
OF OUR COUNTRY WILL BE
A SOURCE OF STRENGTH AND COMFORT
TO OUR GREAT NATION.
GOD BLESS AMERICA.

CHRISTIAN ADAMS
FLIGHT ATTENDANT LORRAINE G. BAY
TODD BEAMER
ALAN BEAVEN
MARK BINGHAM
DEORA BODLEY
FLIGHT ATTENDANT SANDRA W. BRADSHAW
MARION BRITTON
THOMAS BURNETT
WILLIAM CASHMAN
GEORGINE CORRIGAN
PATRICIA CUSHING
CAPTAIN JASON DAHL
JOSEPH DELUCA
PATRICK DRISCOLL
EDWARD FELT
JANE C. FOLGER
COLLEEN FRASER
ANDREW GARCIA
JEREMY GLICK
KRISTIN GOULD
LAUREN GRANDCOLAS
FLIGHT ATTENDANT WANDA A. GREEN
DONALD GREENE
LINDA GRONLUND
RICHARD GUADAGNO
FIRST OFFICER LEROY HOMER
TOSHIYA KUGE
FLIGHT ATTENDANT CEECEE LYLES
HILDA MARCIN
WALESKA MARTINEZ
NICOLE MILLER
LOUIS J. NACKE
JEAN PETERSON
DONALD PETERSON
MARK ROTHENBERG
CHRISTINE SNYDER
JOHN TALIGNANI
HONOR ELIZABETH WAINIO
FLIGHT ATTENDANT DEBORAH A. WELSH

UNITED FLIGHT 93
SEPTEMBER 11, 2001

A memorial plaque dedicated to the people who lost their lives on Flight 93

American Airlines pilot Captain James C. Condes shows his son the 2002 Pentagon memorial at Arlington National Cemetery.

him. When they finished, she heard him ask, "Are you ready, guys?" After a pause, he said, "Let's roll."[3] At that, several other passengers finished phone calls in order to join the group rushing the cockpit.

The passenger revolt began at 9:57 and lasted six minutes. The struggle was captured on the cockpit voice recorder, which was later recovered. As the passengers struggled to get the cockpit door open, Jarrah rolled the plane to knock them off balance. They continued to rush the door. Rather than let the passengers take them over, Jarrah and the other hijackers decided to put the plane down.

On the voice recorder, one of the hijackers can be heard yelling, "Allah is the greatest. Allah is the greatest. Allah is the greatest. Allah is the greatest."[4]

Then nothing.

Flight 93 plowed into an empty field in Shanksville, Pennsylvania, just twenty minutes' flying time from Washington, D.C.

One of the passengers on board Flight 93 was a trained pilot, so perhaps if the passengers had succeeded in taking control of the cockpit, there would have been a sliver of hope for survival. There is no question that their courage in preventing the hijackers from carrying out their mission saved untold lives.

"Now knowing there were a few people on board who showed that level of courage . . . ," Todd Beamer's widow, Lisa, later said. "It's just an inspiration to everybody when there's not a lot of inspiration to go around."[5]

Once the shock of the attacks wore off, anger set in. After the investigation determined that Osama bin Laden was behind the plot, the U.S. government turned its anger on Afghanistan and its Taliban rulers. In a speech, President Bush said that the United States would make no distinction between those who carried out the hijackings and those who harbored and supported them.[6] Since the Taliban allowed bin Laden to operate out of Afghanistan, the decision was made to take military action against Afghanistan. Initially, the stated goal was to root out bin Laden, but ultimately the bombing continued until the Taliban government toppled.

Although several of his top associates had been captured or killed, by 2008 bin Laden remained elusive. It was believed that, if still alive, he was most likely hiding in the mountains that line the Afghanistan-Pakistan border.

Some suspected he was dead, having succumbed to either diabetes or kidney disease. Since he was known to have at least one double, it is impossible to know if the man on the few videotapes sent to the media since September 11, 2001, really is bin Laden or an imposter.

In the months following the attacks, the World Trade Center, or Ground Zero, as it came to be called, attracted hundreds of people every day who paid their respects to those who lost their lives. Determined to improve the nation's security, the government mandated many changes: airport screening was improved; the Department of Homeland Security was created to coordinate federal, state, and local governments to protect citizens and resources; and a national security advisory system was instituted to let citizens know the threat level of terrorist attack. More controversial was President Bush's decision to invade Iraq, which contributed to his earning the lowest approval ratings of any rated U.S. president.

In August 2006, the World Trade Center Memorial Foundation and the Port Authority of New York and New Jersey began construction on the National September 11 Memorial and Museum at the World Trade Center. The memorial, designed by Michael Arad and Peter Walker and called *Reflecting Absence,* would be located on the original World Trade Center site. Where the Twin Towers once stood, water would cascade down the sides of two 30-foot pits that would hold reflecting pools. The names of the victims would be inscribed around the pools. Surrounding the memorial would be Memorial Plaza, filled with oak trees.

The museum, which would also commemorate the victims of the 1993 attack, would contain artifacts retrieved from Ground Zero and would focus on the events of 9/11 and its impact on New Yorkers and the world. Alice Greenwald, the director of the Memorial and Museum, noted, "Ultimately, the story must be about the people affected by this event."[7]

The Taliban were one of the mujahideen, or groups of Muslim "holy warriors," that formed to fight against Afghanistan's Soviet-backed government in the late 1970s. Hoping to retain control, the Afghan leaders asked for Soviet military help. The resulting war lasted almost ten years. After the Soviet military left, the Afghan government could not control the mujahideen, and in 1992 Kabul was captured and the government overthrown. At first, a coalition of mujahideen banded together to form a new government. The alliance quickly fell apart, and soon the different mujahideen turned on each other, beginning a civil war. The fighting left Afghanistan little more than a collection of territories controlled by either mujahideen or warlords.

In late 1994, the Pakistani government hired a group of Taliban to provide security for a trade route between Pakistan and Central Asia. The Taliban emerged as a formidable fighting force and were able to defeat local warlords as well as rival mujahideen. In 1996, the Taliban first captured the city of Kandahar, then in September captured Kabul and took over leadership of the country. After so many years of war, the majority of Afghans were relieved to see a decrease in fighting, regardless of who was running the country—even if it meant living under a very strict interpretation of Islamic laws.

Led by Mullah Muhammad Omar, the Taliban managed to eliminate a lot of corruption, but conditions in the cities remained poor, with high unemployment and food shortages. However, the Taliban became best known, and notorious, for their support of terrorists, their harsh treatment of women, and their overall restrictive laws. Public executions and whippings held in large soccer stadiums were regular events.

The Taliban offered Osama bin Laden and members of Al-Qaeda refuge and allowed them to run training camps in Afghanistan. It is believed that Omar married one of bin Laden's daughters. After the September 11 terrorist attacks, the United States demanded the Taliban turn over bin Laden. When they refused, the U.S. began bombing Taliban military

Taliban fighters in Herat in July 2001

sites and helping the Northern Alliance, who wanted to overthrow the Taliban. By December, the Taliban was ousted from power. In October 2004, Afghanistan held its first democratic presidential elections.

Chapter Notes

Chapter 1. An Unusually Beautiful Day . . .

1. BBC News Interactive: Interview with Gedeon and Jules Naudet, September 11, 2002, http://news.bbc.co.uk/1/shared/spl/hi/world/02/september_11/forum/txt/naudet_transcript.txt

2. NPR, *Timeline for United Flight 175*, http://www.npr.org/templates/story/story.php?storyId=1962517

Chapter 2. The Making of a Terrorist

1. Chris Hedges, "Sudan Linked to Rebellion In Algeria," *New York Times*, December 24, 1994, http://query.nytimes.com/gst/fullpage.html?res=9C01E4D71F38F937A15751C1A962958260&scp=1&sq=%22wealthy+Saudi+financier+who+bankrolls+Islamic+militant+groups+from+Algeria+to+Saudi+Arabia%22&st=nyt

2. Robert McFadden, "Bin Laden's Journey from Rich, Pious Boy to the Mask of Evil," *New York Times*, September 30, 2001, http://query.nytimes.com/gst/fullpage.html?res=9C01E7D9143DF933A0575AC0A9679C8B63

3. Muslim Brothers ("The Brothers"), http://www.fas.org/irp/world/para/mb.htm

Chapter 3. Jihad

1. BBC On This Day, 26 February— "1993: World Trade Center Bomb Terrorizes New York," http://news.bbc.co.uk/onthisday/hi/dates/stories/february/26/newsid_2516000/2516469.stm

2. PBS.org, Online Newshour: "Al-Qaeda's Fatwa," February 23, 1998, http://www.pbs.org/newshour/terrorism/international/fatwa_1998.html

3. Cornell University Law School, U.S. Code Collection: Transportation Security Administration http://www.law.cornell.edu/uscode/html/uscode49/usc_sec_49_00000114----000-.html#h_2

Chapter 4. Uncommon Heroism

1. David Ignatius, Book Review: "*The Book on Terror*," *Washington Post*, July 30, 2004, http://www.washingtonpost.com/wp-dyn/articles/A26729-2004Jul30.html

2. "Accounts from the South Tower," *New York Times*, May 26, 2002, http://www.mishalov.com/wtc_southtower.html

3. Ibid.

4. Nancy Gibbs, "Special Report: The Day of the Attack." *Time*, September 12, 2001, http://www.time.com/time/world/article/0,8599,174655,00.html

Chapter 5. Fighting Back

1. Josh Tyrangiel, Michele Orecklin, James Poniewozik, John Cloud, Jodie Morse, Amanda Ripley, Ellin Martens, et al. "Facing the End." *Time*, September 24, 2001, http://www.time.com/time/magazine/article/0,9171,1000882-1,00.html

2. Ibid.

3. Newsweek.com, "The Road to September 11," October 1, 2001, http://www.newsweek.com/id/75524

4. CBSNews.com, "Flight 93 Tape Airs At Moussaoui Trial," April 12, 2006, http://www.cbsnews.com/stories/2006/04/12/terror/main1491489.shtml

5. Charles Lane, Don Phillips, and David Snyder. "A Sky Filled with Chaos, Uncertainty and True Heroism." *Washington Post*, September 17, 2001; p. A03.

6. Serge Schmemann. "U.S. Attacked; President Vows to Exact Punishment for 'Evil.' " *New York Times*, September 12, 2001, http://query.nytimes.com/gst/fullpage.html?res=9403E6D81238F931A2575AC0A9679C8B63

7. "Construction Starts on World Trade Center Memorial," *Voices of America*. August 31, 2006, http://www.voanews.com/english/archive/2006-08/2006-08-31-voa66.cfm

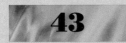

Chronology

1928   Muslim Brotherhood is founded.

1957   Osama bin Laden is born in Saudi Arabia.

1966   Construction begins on World Trade Center.

1968   Bin Laden inherits part of the family fortune after father dies in plane crash.

1970   North Tower, also called 1 World Trade Center, opens in December.

1972   South Tower, or 2 World Trade Center, opens in January.

1979   Soviet Union invades Afghanistan.

1984   Bin Laden and Azzam form Maktab Al-Khidamat (Office of Services).

1988   Al-Qaeda is formed; months later, Azzam is assassinated.

1991   Bin Laden moves to Sudan.

1992   A hotel in Yemen is bombed; it is later believed to be Al-Qaeda's first attack.

1993   A car bomb detonates in the World Trade Center parking basement on February 26.

1996   Bin Laden is expelled from Sudan and goes to Afghanistan.

1998   Bin Laden calls on Muslims to kill Americans. U.S. embassies in Kenya and Tanzania are bombed.

2001   Twin Towers are destroyed and the Pentagon is damaged in terrorist attack on September 11. Hijackers on a fourth plane are foiled when passengers fight back over fields in Pennsylvania. President George W. Bush declares war on terror. On October 7, the United States launches air attacks against the Taliban. Bush signs the controversial USA PATRIOT Act (Uniting and Strengthening America by Providing Appropriate Tools Required to Intercept and Obstruct Terrorism Act of 2001). In December, the Taliban is ousted from power in Afghanistan.

2004   The National Commission on Terrorist Attacks Upon the United States (9/11 Commission) issues its final report on the attacks. Democratic elections are held in Afghanistan.

2006   The newly rebuilt 7 World Trade Center opens in May. Construction begins on National September 11 Memorial & Museum at the World Trade Center.

2008   Zacarias Moussaoui appeals his guilty plea and subsequent life sentence in February.

Timeline in History

1948   Israel is founded as the world's only Jewish State.

1967   Israel is victorious in Six-Day War against Egypt, Jordan, and Syria.

1970   Yasir Arafat is appointed supreme commander of the Palestine Liberation Army, organized to create a state for Palestinian Arabs in the Middle East.

1979   Iranian students take over U.S. embassy November 4 and take 52 Americans hostage.

1985   The cruise ship *Achille Lauro* is hijacked by four Palestinians in October.

1989   Berlin Wall falls.

1990   Nelson Mandela is freed from prison in South Africa.

1995   Alfred P. Murrah Federal Building in Oklahoma City is bombed April 19; Timothy McVeigh is later convicted and executed for planting the bomb. Israeli Prime Minister Yitzhak Rabin is assassinated on November 4.

2000   Al-Qaeda sends two suicide bombers to attack the USS *Cole* in Aden, Yemen; the explosion kills seventeen U.S. servicemen.

2004   A massive tsunami in the Indian Ocean on December 26 kills over 220,000 people in Asia.

2006   The revised Patriot Act, a temporary law devised to aid investigators route out terrorism, becomes permanent.

2008   All the defendants convicted in the attack of the USS *Cole* in Yemen have escaped from prison or been freed by Yemeni officials.

A model of the World Trade Center memorial *Reflecting Absence*, designed by Michael Arad and Peter Walker

Further Reading

For Young Readers

Frank, Mitch. *Understanding September 11th: Answering Questions about the Attacks on America*. New York: Viking Juvenile, 2005.

Hampton, Wilborn. *September 11, 2001: Attack on New York City*. Cambridge, Massachusetts: Candlewick, 2007.

Osborne, Mary Pope. *New York's Bravest*. New York: Knopf Books for Young Readers, 2002.

Wheeler, Jill C. *September 11, 2001: The Day That Changed America*. Minnesota: ABDO & Daughters, 2002.

Works Consulted

"Accounts from the South Tower." *New York Times*, May 26, 2002. http://www.mishalov.com/wtc_southtower.html

BBC News Interactive http://news.bbc.co.uk/1/shared/spl/hi/world/02/september_11/forum/txt/naudet_transcript.txt

BBC: On This Day, World Trade Center Bomb Terrorizes New York, http://news.bbc.co.uk/onthisday/hi/dates/stories/february/26/newsid_2516000/2516469.stm

Beamer, Lisa, and Ken Abraham. *Let's Roll: Finding Hope in the Midst of Crisis*. Carol Stream, Illinois: Tyndale House Publishers, 2002.

Bennett, William J. *Why We Fight: Moral Clarity and the War on Terrorism*. New York: Doubleday, 2002.

CBSNews.com, "Flight 93 Tape Airs at Moussaoui Trial" http://www.cbsnews.com/stories/2006/04/12/terror/main1491489.shtml

"Construction Starts on World Trade Center Memorial," *Voices of America*. August 31, 2006, http://www.voanews.com/english/archive/2006-08/2006-08-31-voa66.cfm

Cornell University Law School, U.S. Code Collection, http://www.law.cornell.edu/uscode/html/us code49/usc_sec_49_00000114----000-.html#h_2

Gibbs, Nancy. "Special Report: The Day of the Attack." *Time*, Sept 12, 2001, http://www.time.com/time/world/article/0,8599,174655,00.html

Global Security—Homeland Security: 9-11 http://www.globalsecurity.org/security/profiles/9-11.htm

Halberstam, David. *Firehouse*. New York: Hyperion, 2002.

Hedges, Chris. "Sudan Linked to Rebellion in Algeria." *New York Times*, December 24, 1994, http://query.nytimes.com/gst/fullpage.html?res=9C01E4D71F38F937A15751C1A962958260&scp=1&sq=%22wealthy+Saudi+financier+who+bankrolls+Islamic+militant+groups+from+Algeria+to+Saudi+Arabia%22&st=nyt

Intelligence Resource Program http://www.fas.org/irp/world/para/mb.htm

Kornbluth, Jesse, and Jessica Papin, editors. *Because We Are Americans: What We Discovered on September 11, 2001*. New York: Warner Books, 2001.

Lane, Charles, Don Phillips, and David Snyder. "A Sky Filled With Chaos, Uncertainty and True Heroism." *Washington Post*, September 17, 2001; p. A03.

Lutnick, Howard, and Tom Barbash. *On Top of the World: Cantor Fitzgerald and 9/11: A Story of Loss and Renewal*. New York: HarperCollins, 2002.

McCourt, Frank. *Brotherhood*. New York: Sterling Publications, 2001.

McFadden, Robert. "Bin Laden's Journey from Rich, Pious Boy to the Mask of Evil." *New York Times*. September 30, 2001. http://query.nytimes.com/gst/fullpage.html?res=9C01E7D9143DF933A0575AC0A9679C8B63

Newsweek.com: The Road to September 11 http://www.newsweek.com/id/75524

NPR: 9/11 Hearings, http://www.npr.org/911hearings/

PBS.org: Online Newshour: Al-Qaeda's 1998 Fatwa, http://www.pbs.org/newshour/terrorism/international/fatwa_1998.html

Tyrangiel, Josh, Michele Orecklin, James Poniewozik, John Cloud, Jodie Morse, Amanda Ripley, Ellin Martens. "Facing the End." *Time*, September 24, 2001 http://www.time.com/time/magazine/article/0,9171,1000882-1,00.html

On the Internet

BBC News, America's Day of Terror http://news.bbc.co.uk/hi/english/static/in_depth/americas/2001/day_of_terror/

CNN.com, September 11: A Memorial http://www.cnn.com/SPECIALS/2001/memorial/

September 11 Digital Archive, http://911digitalarchive.org/

Glossary

coalition (koh-uh-LIH-shun)—A temporary alliance of parties or countries for a particular purpose.

fatwa (FAHT-wah)—A legal decision or decree made by an Islamic religious leader.

gentrify (JEN-trih-fy)—To renew or rebuild an area in order to attract wealthier classes and therefore more money.

indicted (in-DY-ted)—Formally charged with a crime.

jihad (JEE-hod)—A Muslim holy war fought against non-Muslims.

mujahideen (muh-jah-hih-DEEN)—Islamic guerrilla fighters who take up arms for a religious cause.

transponder (trans-PON-der)—A radar or radio transmitter that responds to signals from another radar or radio set; it is used for identifying and locating aircraft and other types of vehicles.

ulema (oo-leh-MAA)—Body of mullahs, Muslim officials trained in religious law.

Design of the new Freedom Tower

Index